ADDITIONAL PRAISE FOR *RARE FUEL*

These days I'm smiling more / broadly, swaying with the palm / trees. With each trip around / the sun, there's a more profound / patina on our prospects, / a soul-surface that blinds me to the limits of setting / our sights, where each of us / who had failed to kill / ourselves learned to live. In *Rare Fuel*, **Rex Wilder** is the Virgil who guides us through the underworld of his own personal hell, ———— killed him. With utter candor, Wilder describes hi— from the brink of self-annihilation and back to this most about these poems is that he finds a way to giv **do you describe the mind unmoored, the soul d this, in a collection that will leave you shaken**— beautiful book.

— **George Bilgere**, Distinguished Professor of English at John _____

Rex Wilder makes words unveil feelings, and his poems are new and surprising while hewing to traditional forms. He writes about serious mental illness with sly wit, unfolding meaning, and unsentimental pathos. **This collection is generous and universal—embracing the world with all its trials and triumphs and grounding us in memory, recollection, and joy;** as he writes in "Recipe," "It will get dark with or without us / but without us, I won't care."
— **Katherine Howell**, Literary Editor, *National Review*

In **Rex Wilder**'s poems, his "traumatized heart" beats with troubled and tenacious language. **Excruciating experiences toward self-worth and sanity keep the reader rapt, awaiting an uneasy affirmation of "peaceable suspense."** These are honest poems of perseverance, seeking clarity and calm while his cri de coeur persists.
— **Susan Kinsolving**, winner of the Poetry Society of America's Lyric Poetry Award and finalist for The National Book Critics Circle Award

Honestly, as a psychiatrist and a human, I would read anything Rex Wilder writes. In these penetrating, intimate poems, the author courageously chronicles a dark night of the soul depression, his inpatient stay in a psychiatric facility, and breathtaking emergence into the light. I applaud Rex as a powerful role model for others on similar journeys as they grow in ways that will uplift their souls. Highly recommended.
— **Judith Orloff**, MD, New York Times bestselling author of *The Genius of Empathy*

In *Rare Fuel*, by **Rex Wilder**, a severe illness leads to reparation, even wholeness, in language that is fresh and lyrical, and in an original use of classical forms. After recovery, the poet gains wisdom and shares it with us all. There's a new music in many of his lines: "every song / begins in song's absence," in "looking is no substitute for seeing, / And only illness can startle love into being," "this strain of love, its stain," "the high note / only a lover can bear" or "I laugh / at the Church of I Guess. / I have nothing to confess." "Canal Nocturne" is a sensitive, original take on the pandemic. **The book rings with the exhilaration of freedom from the chains of confinement.**
— **Grace Schulman**, author of *Again, the Dawn: New and Selected Poems* and winner of the *Frost Medal for Distinguished Lifetime Achievement in Poetry*

RARE FUEL

WINNER OF THE
DONNA WOLF-PALACIO POETRY PRIZE

poems by

Rex Wilder

Finishing Line Press
Georgetown, Kentucky

RARE FUEL

*WINNER OF THE
DONNA WOLF-PALACIO POETRY PRIZE*

I check in but don't check out, twice in one month.

The first time I was virgin, the second was no surprise.

I take showers and shits so the attendant can sort of see me.

I have traded in my free will for costly safety.

A schedule for the day hangs above a puzzle on a table.

Attendants read our rights to themselves.

The thick windows do not open by design.

They're so thick we can't hear the ambulances approach.

Patients arrive with sirens dripping off their shoulders.

Thunder cannot completely shrug lightning.

Copyright © 2024 by Rex Wilder
ISBN 979-8-88838-790-0 First Edition
All rights reserved under International and Pan-American Copyright Conventions. No part of this book may be reproduced in any manner whatsoever without written permission from the publisher, except in the case of brief quotations embodied in critical articles and reviews.

Publisher: Leah Huete de Maines
Editor: Christen Kincaid
Cover Art and Design: Rex Wilder
Author Photo: Robert Sallin

Order online: www.finishinglinepress.com
also available on amazon.com

Author inquiries and mail orders:
Finishing Line Press
PO Box 1626
Georgetown, Kentucky 40324
USA

Contents

The Mad Boy 1
A Forest Tale 2
The Ruminate Room 3
Balance 4
Welcome to Mad 5
The Banana Split of History 6
To One Not Ill 7
To This Pink Pearl Eraser 8
▣
Not a Week Goes By 10
The Normy Cheer 11
Four Moons 12
Mother Birds 13
▣
Rooster) 15
Proud Horses and Let Glory Come 16
Lenox Hill 17
Weightless 18
In Praise of Disorder 19
▣
Werewolf 21
The Peanut Butter Party 22
The Marine Layer 23
Johnny Late Comely 24
To Louie 25
▣
This Carrier 27
▣
Dolphins On Glass 30
Canal Nocturne 31
I'll Explain Another Time 32
Bananas In Isolation 33
Hard Labor 34
Two Harbors 35
Fifth Column 36
▣
Corner Circle 38

A Corto di Eternità 39
Eye-Broom Sonnet 40
Hear Back 41
◘
Balking, He) 43
Brain) 44
Corrected) 45
Self-Portrait for All Our Selves 46
◘
And Now I'm Sane 48
Zoo 49
Surviving Son As Gravedigger 50
Energy 51
Normy Starts With No 52
◘
Old Patient as the Last of the Great Magazines 54
Recipe 55
Isn't That Crazy? 56
See You in the Funny Papers 57
◘
The Snows of No Country 59
Spending Lies 60
Summer Break 61
Canyon Morning 62
Canyon Market 63
Glasses, with Bird 64
◘
Envoi 1 66
Envoi 2 67
Envoi 3 68
Envoi 4 69
Envoi 5 70
Envoi 6 71
Envoi 7 72
Envoi 8 73
◘
Writing You Now 76
The Prayer Sonnet 77
Red-Tailed Hawk 78
Set Free 79

for

*Sanam Abrishami, Hannah Bergenfield, Anastasia Boissier,
Judy Briskin, Bernard Briskin, Ansley Calandra, Cody Cassano,
Alex Coleman, Natalie Wong Dobrott, Antonela Balaguer Escobar,
Richard Gilbert, Sydney Goldstein, Taylor Harris, Aimee Michelle Haynes,
Jessica Hornik, Olivia Kerns, Corinne Louise, Ben Mandeberg,
Michael McGarry, Madeline Kahan McNamara, Robert Sallin,
Dr. Edward Share, Randy Sheinbein, Kendall Smith, Logan Stanislaw,
Grace Starbird, Madeline Trachtenberg, Miles Trump, Josh Wilcox,
Cam Wilder, Kellianne Wilder, Oliver Wilder, Simon Wilder,
Marianna Wong, and Julia Young,*

to whom I owe my life

The Mad Boy

"You don't know where he's been."
everyone's best friend

Diagnoses came like storm cells on a radar in a drought.

With blood at the lip, the angels laughed last.
Good luck befell them despite
Their singular trauma. As land masses,
They inflated roses, drank from stained window glasses,
And plucked boys and girls from thinnest air.

A fuller world tuned to the beauty of their first sacrifice,
And turned to it. Meanwhile I, stammering umlauted
Rëx, laughed first: Drawing the exile straw, I was banished
Among hordes of The Fallible, leaving Prologue's gates
Swinging on rusted hinges.
                          A one-nut Diaspora I was. I was
Also jostled and made numb. Such was my ethical
Anesthetic that I could not mitigate the pain and insecurity
I might have caused the angels by suffering myself.
In one snowy month, I lost feeling altogether.

Curiously I could feel this happening,
Though why no tingles?
Think mice in slow motion scattering in a barn fire.
Think them not running fast enough.

A Forest Tale

Not some monster in the woods behind the cedar—
No, I see it's a deer and I feed her

All I have, my love of nature, imagine she's chewing
On it. Neither of us is musical, but we two sing

Or hum. We beat on our limitations. *I have been
A good son,* I tell her over tears. *I have been

A good deer* is her response, as if I'd surprised
Her not with my desperation, but my disguise.

The Ruminate Room

In an hour it'll be day,
The fatigue of dawn
When you can't go on.
—Or you can,
Like the bill on a toucan.
I feel like I've woken
On a raft in the middle
Of a lake deep
Into a summer afternoon.
Paddle to shore,
Paddle to shore.
The scrawl of thoughts trailing
Behind me
Hope's signature.

Balance

Dishes have been shattering   in my brain since April.
I have been shattering, too,   but what passes for plates
Inside my head thuds almost   silently, like roadkill
Heaven-sent (soft, fleshy rhythms)   down the interstates.
My brain's too small for my skull   since I fell ill
And rattles when I'm rattled.   Sometimes I'm sure
I'm thinking rationally,   as if I've opened an umbrella
From a pink cocktail and   *feel* dry, *feel* cured.
The space between letters   vanishes without a word.

Welcome to Mad

My brain gambols through meadows.
The softest affections are like precious metals,
Valuable, tender, stupid as fruit in a bowl.
Each day I grow more convinced my scrawl

Is easy as a primer and destined to be read
In some waiting room on Olympus and spread
To the gods' group sessions lower down.
I'm not manic, but methodical in my clown-

Car want. A tree could be a ladder I could climb
To the showerhead of a quenched storm,
A glass of milk the antidote to thirst
For all animals and failures in love, last and first.

Fall forward, arms open, to embrace
My new kind. It's like a plane returning to base.
Just the press of our bodies against depression,
The mountains crinkled like the blue drapes of heaven.

The Banana Split of History

From now on, I can count on nothing that
Makes sense and begin to take matters into my own
Hands, one of which is held over a traumatized
Heart. I pledge allegiance. Imagine if every machine
That requires fossil fuel shut off at the same time;
You'd hear birds sing, sharply and maybe even,
If you leaned in, the mechanical slosh of flower
Buds crying out for sun and rain. We nut cases,
Who don't Noah better, launch ourselves two-
By-two, in blue hospital garb instead of bathing
Suits, rhyming with each other like we're baking
Patty cakes beside a red resort canoe the color
Of our warm blood's lake. The waters of our affections
Are impossibly deep, yet we never see the bottom.
Even on suicide day, we never think about jumping.

To One Not Ill

Sorry to be so weighty;
It's luckier to be light,
Like cotton candy. Shady,
This business of white
Lying. Hell, hello cut short,
And pulls me into port.
Whither hello, matey?
The reach of *yes* is *maybe*
Now. I even sip grey tea
As I sugarcoat this fight.

To This Pink Pearl Eraser

Your body pink and prehensile
Evokes childbirth for this man.
Could you ever be a witch's brew
For my magical thinking?—
As if such were still proffered
To the mad. What story in my life
Needs to be rubbed out, which
Shivers me with gangster justice?
These are only my notes.
What vanity do you have
In a world that was originally penciled in,
Before words bled with color?
Eraser dust must be its own
Delicate revision, which I take
To be mine now. Do you hone
Or merely make my sadness
Look silly, with all its curlicues?
Your Achilles heel has deep
Feelings for my plight, which
Is like a dinner plate. You and I
Are finished, either way.

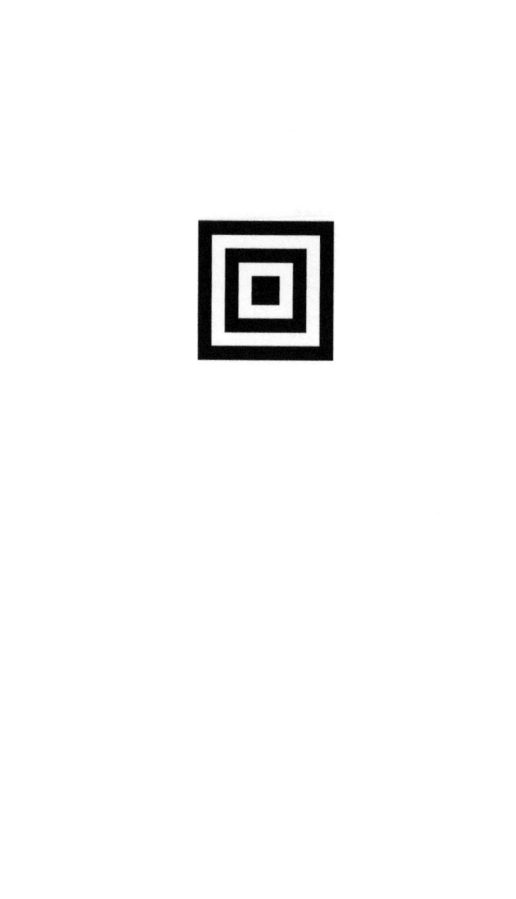

Not A Week Goes By

Not a week goes by in treat-
Ment without my wondering
How I became that creep,
A kind of solo lover blundering

Through the human showroom
Desperate to experience
His life any way but alone,
His unintentional prurience

A source of shame. A glint
Of sun flashes from a window
Four floors up. We can't
See inside from this far below.

The Normy Cheer

("Normy" meant to those of us at the hospital:
any person out in the real world. As in "not us.")

Normy, Normy, pudding and pie
Why be normal any more?
Hand on Cheek, Head on Thigh
Hold each other, watch the door.
Hath you Plath, a Daddy dear?
Shiver me love, into the river
If I don't jump will you deliver?
Whiter water makes better bait.
Plunging for the deadly lake—
No such thing as bad mistakes
Cascading toward the cataract.
So peaceful how we swirl over.
We are each each other's lover.
Head on Breast, Feet in Touch;
Pores open to love by lunch.
Untie the knot in Do Not Enter.
Feel, Feel! at the healing center,
I'm origami now so fold me.
Hold me, cold me. Slide in sex.
What's hard is Rex, the dirty
Shame, blind years removed.
Tumble lovers till we're loved.
Normy, Normy, pie and pudding
Pistil, stamen, roses budding.

Four Moons

There are eleven moons, I'm told,
New moon through old,
As there were eleven suicides,
Failures all, still alive,
Walking up and down my ward.
Being a moon is hard.

Being a moon is hard,
Having to be starred
Yet making the heavens faint;
A single coat of black paint
That barely lasts the night.
A moon has an appetite.

A moon has an appetite.
Without a mooring in sight
It yearns for a familiar
Anchor on Earth, a streetcar
To ride on, a cul-de-sac—
A woman with a moon-hat!

A woman with a moon-hat
At the window, I remember that.
Doctors sautéed her brain.
She became a fixture; a ribbon
Of pain shone blue in her hair.
The moon is beyond repair.

Mother Birds

We were like mother birds
Feeding other mother birds.
But perhaps the saddest story
Was the society woman who
Stopped believing in herself;
She never stopped thanking
Me for the lantern I carried
In my eyes, then died swinging
Like a censer. Despite my own
Limits, my friends had me
Thinking I'm a guardian angel
Myself. Maybe we all are.

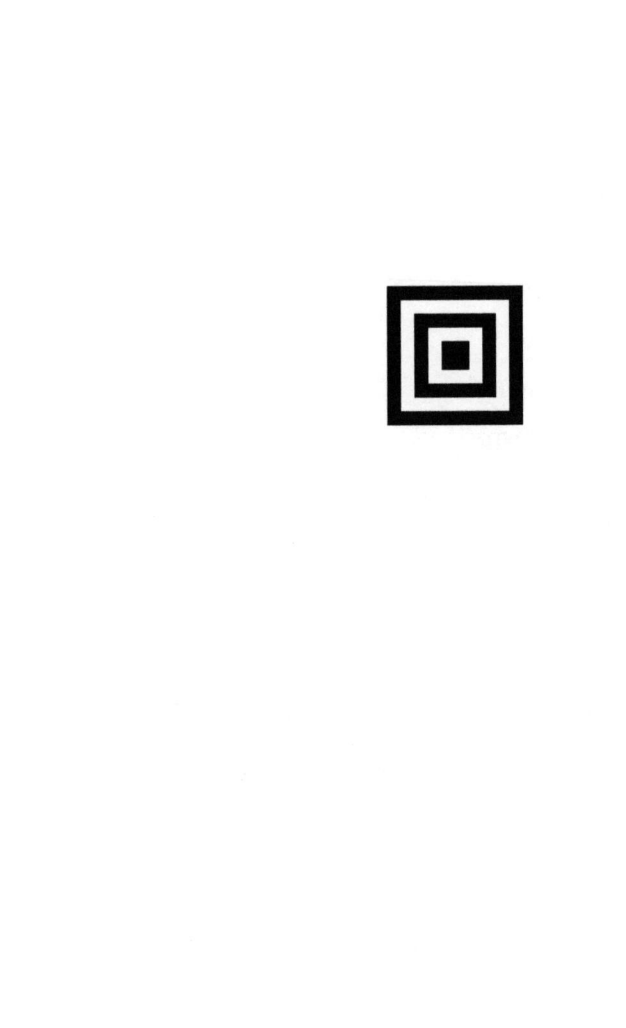

Rooster)

Rooster
mornings in the psych ward. Here she comes
to crow, my favorite nurse and
booster.

Proud Horses and Let Glory Come

The disparity between murk like a stable's
And the day's usual glare. It's a love fest
Of illumination, a demonstration, a convention
Sponsored by Universal Refulgence on
Hospital grounds, where luster is the best
Case scenario. The group leader is right.
No one has ever brought darkness into a room.

Lenox Hill

    11 months ago she
    decided not to take
Suicide's side
    and cut herself down
before her neck could break.
In the ambulance she peed
    herself and puked.
She wished she could have
    thrown up her brain.
For her brain's sake.
    Touch and go between
sirens and the rain.
        Her heart's foot
    pumping the brake.

Weightless

The Italian astronaut confesses in her memoir
That weightless, she felt an otherworldly
Sexuality. Every part of her body had equal
Pull: no dragging down or up. Out,
Infinitely. The treatment center seeks a centering
Like this. One body in delicious, unpredictable
Flux and continuous flower. Or eighty-three
In search of oneness. Twirling among comets,
Choreographing, unmoored. Orianna knows
That feeling, the best chapters tell me, when boundaries
Are like bouffants: almost comical, silly shows,
Never forbidding. She never took a walk into space
But longs to articulate the desire of a human
For the stars' worship: nil, annihilating.
Not forged in the crucible of darkness but forsaken there.
I remember holding my weightless head
In place, in the hospital's lockdown, feeling
I had to calibrate or die.

In Praise Of Disorder

It's not until we're deranged
That we discern our brain's many parts,
Which can now be rearranged.

Think of any war.
After it's over, the rubble shows what we're willing
To die for.

Werewolf

Squeaky silent. Old cries for help scrubbed clean.
It's not news that there's peace in surrender,
But home seems as far away as a steno pool.
I marvel at the courage of the nurses, who don't seem
To realize I could rip flesh from their bones
And eat them, meds, syringes, and all for a midnight
Snack. Gotta love that full moon. They just smile,
Or don't smile, as they make their rounds,
Reflected or distorted in the thickest windows
You've ever seen, or seen through. Maybe I'll waltz
Into the hall in my asylum-issued grey socks,
Investigate the view, which I am. I *am* the view.

The Peanut Butter Party

It's party therapy, a supervised Fourth of July
For patients who are sick in the head.
Grownups eating peanut butter and jelly,

A petting zoo, too. It's all pretty silly.
We're being watched like baking bread.
It's party therapy, a supervised Fourth of July

In the parking lot. Balloons like big bellies.
One rule: No hugging, the director said.
Grownups eating peanut butter and jelly

And cups of sparkling Martinelli's
Is evidently the opposite of suicide.
It's part therapy, this supervised Fourth of July

Where fireworks shine in the eyes of a billy
Goat, though he slops around in the mud.
Hey, little goat—want some peanut butter and jelly?

A year ago, sober, our tears were of joy;
Now, sad, can't cry because of a med.
It's party therapy, a supervised Fourth of July.
Grownups eating peanut butter and jelly.

The Marine Layer

The morning is a bathtub to crown with mist.

Out of my element,
I enjoy the privileges of a guest.
My own plus-one.

Will I bathe in the sun?
Cloud judgment, Rex; there's no place for discernment
In love.

Waiting awhile before I dry off.

Johnny Late Comely

"I might not be here when you get back,"
She says like she's a bouquet.
It's quite a trick to stay on track

In love so don't turn your back
On your cellmate, okay?
She might not be there when you get back.

Obviously. You don't need an almanac
To plant the seed of doubt today.
It's quite a trick to stay on track

When you're riding on one rail, Jack—
No matter what you say,
And she could leave before you get back.

Listen *cuh-clack cuh-clack cuh-clack*
To your heart and do not stray.
It's quite a trick to stay on track,

Like finding hay in a needle stack.
Johnny, don't go out to play.
She might not be here when you get back.
Stay (may I?) on love's shiny track.

To Louie

Off leash at last.
You were tugging just this morning.
Let my eyes flag at half-mast,
And my leash hand rise in mourning,
Weightless now.
Up and down, in and out, why and how.
In your death I flail,
Battered by the recent past.
Dog-speed, my friend.
I will say your name often.
Your nicknames, too.
I like to think if they reach you
In the great above
Or some deep hole
Your absence has dug,
Your funny ears will catch my love
And I will wag my tail.

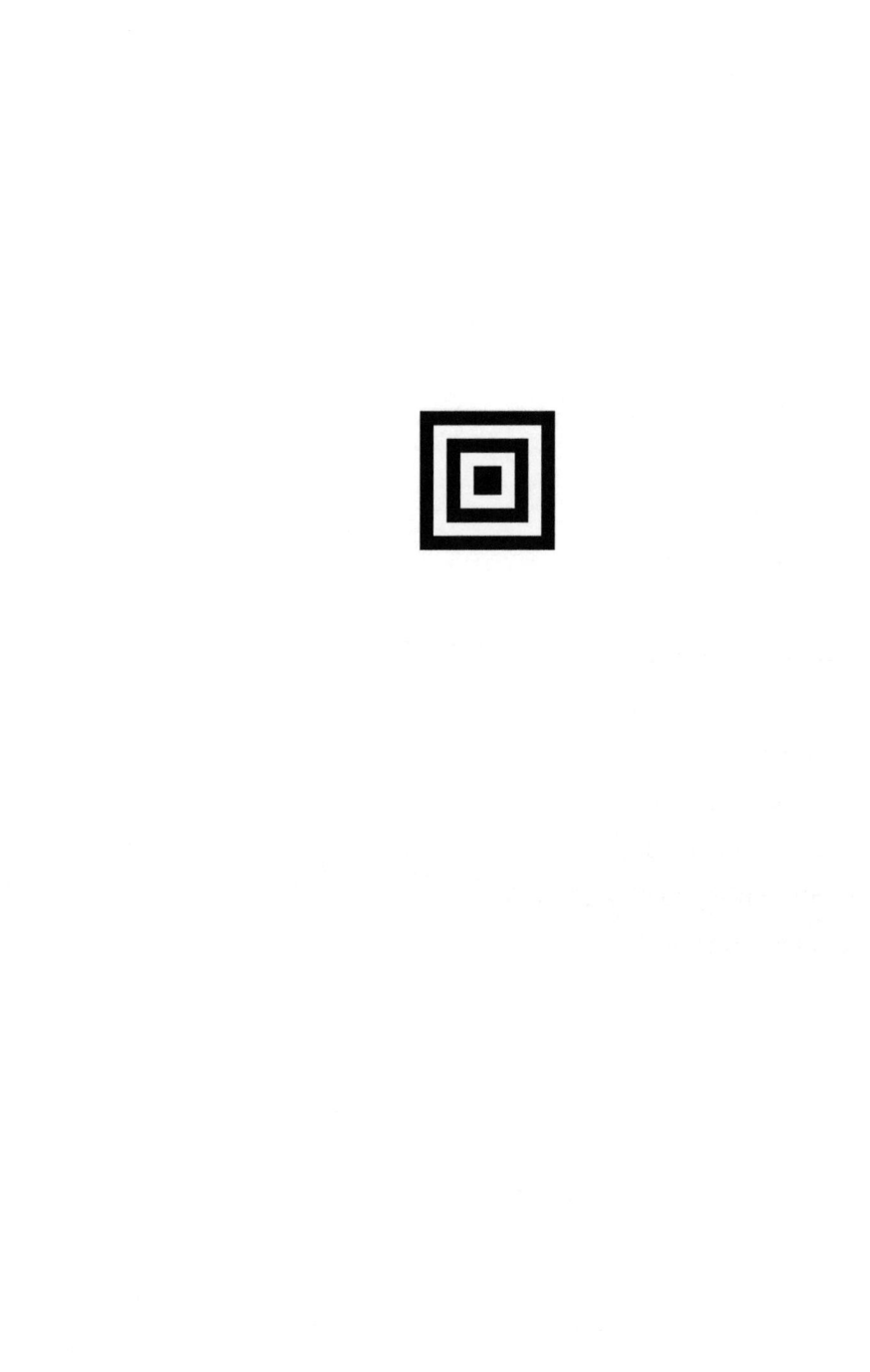

This Carrier

Returning from the war after the rains
As the reigns like swords soared down
I thought of their desert provenance,

The easy etymology of Egypt, though I flew—
Or one could say sailed, wing on wing—
Over Korean waters and the white caps

Of Japan. It was a diversity of adversity.
This would be my last flight before
The final one, which would be from Lahaina,

In ashes. No one crashes over seas, not
Even these seas; just ask this junior-grade
Typhoon. It's a reunion, where droughts

Of doubts are doused. It's my childhood
Garden, where the puddling lakes,
The pop-ups that drew lines of bees,

Had little time to reflect. They were pudding
In the lawn just yesterday. The solid world
Green with its own envy. The stolid curled

In their beds like lima beans, too witless
To bear witness. The rest of us, we ran out
In the yard as if after the morning papers.

Remember the splotchy headlines, I asked
My co-pilot, that paved the snails' interstate,
The golden journalism, the rubber band

That sold the secrecy of the news, the butterflies
That fluttered in each monarch's heart?
No, of course not. He was no older than I

And had died in battle, shot from the sky
Like the photographs sunsets took of us
On our bivouac weekends after the rains

Cleared. Abels, Cains, and Adams drip
Even now from the eaves of our promotion,
This one to peace, this band of bothers

(The *r* buried in my heart!) waving arms
As if you, oh mother and my father,
Were not yet ghosts dressed up as angels,

Coming in to land on this carrier, my life.

Dolphins On Glass

The dolphins I behold out my picture
Window come in twos or threes,
Like bunkmates. They're a fixture
Of this sea-gazing life. Zombies

Or mourners? I can't tell
If they're crying in an ocean
Pre-soaked with tears. Economical
In their not-leaping motion,

They seem to be half-sleeping, wholly
At ease. It's almost holy.

Canal Nocturne

A walk through a canal at a time when most people are home
And not a cloud in the sky nor in the sky's reflection on the water
But there is a difference and only I am there to notice:

The water-sky is a denser color by far than the dry sky above,
Which is the real world, bleached out by lights and virus,
Studded with sounds and filled from every corner with threats

Without and within. Only harmless crabs and sea slugs,
Silhouettes and shadows, tenant the three feet deep. A few fish mill,
Narrowly realize themselves. This is not the first night I've noticed

Looking down that several stars have shone that did not twinkle above,
Weren't there at all. For all the real in reality, experience
Tells me this reflection is what our embracing arms were made for;

For weeks, we have been advised not to hug, nay *ordered*.
Just as even the most cold-blooded of us felt the need.
This morning, CNN announced even an innocent exhale can kill.

We are stranded, too near each other to breathe.

I'll Explain Another Time

How do you fly, I ask
The hummingbird. *I'll explain another
Time,* says the apple at
The moment
It lets go. Waves disappoint like
Fireworks, alike save to those
Who live to measure. Why should I
Think of you across the country
This morning, my friend, in your kayak
On the kill so early in the season?
I wish you were here
To reel me back in, once again,
From the standoffish deeps.
How can any one night possibly wash
This many shells ashore,
That once held a small creature's
Version of love?

Bananas In Isolation

I'm what they call isolating. A bowl of splotched
Bananas for company. They're still attached
To each other, spooning by nature, as if laying
Out on resort lounges, doing their own thing.
So even if they could think it wouldn't be of me.
"Hold me" is an almost chin-up to "Love me,"
A starter plea. I squeeze one of the bananas
In my hand, stupid stupid stupid, and manage
To cry while the sickly yellow skin splits in five
Places and flesh squishes out. I am still alive.

Hard Labor

A chrysanthemum petal makes me think of a swapped
Prisoner. What was given up for this beauty pressing
Against the marble countertop like a face? My country
Regularly brings an innocent home in return for cold
Blood, an art teacher for an assassin. A bottle of sky-
Blue Windex stands by the photo frame by the bananas
Like a guard. Prisoners clean their own cells, I'm told.
To wit, I feel your soft hand on mine as I shine the glass
At all hours, removing the smudge of our separated lives.

Two Harbors

When I started to talk to myself again
It was a good thing
Because I'm fascinating:
I know what I like to hear, and when.

It happened when I got out of bed,
Wobbly from trazodone,
Looking for my phone.
Only the dogs heard what I said.

This brought back the hell of July,
When I hiked every chance
I got, talked to plants
And deer. I didn't want to die.

Life's an audition, you see.
As I make my bed,
Take another med,
I repeat what I said: "Will it be me?"

This cove and that eucalyptus tree,
Buffaloes, a herd of three,
Help me fit my soliloquy
To the undefeated affect of the sea.

Fifth Column

I'd bury this in the Living
Section, giving

It the short shrift the inconstancy
Of its truth deserves. Fancy-

Pants feelings: yawn.
Venice pier at dawn.

My mood lifts
And the fog shifts—

Or is it the other way around?
The sea looks ironed

This morning; or ill.
My heart is close to still.

I can't make love wearing
Nakedness over worry.

Corner Circle

Our hands recently knew violence,
Our hands have grasped at straws.
Our backs comfort threadbare pillows,

Our backs are against the wall.
High windows let us see little,
Though reflections off metal

And shadows from the street
Flash like the promise of flight
And give the lie to our defeat.

A Corto Di Eternità

I hold you now because I won't be able
To hold you then, after the dessert of our lives.
A love poem is like hot food on a table,

Especially when you're hungry. There's a timetable.
The best part's when the waiter arrives.
I hold you now because I won't be able

To wrap my arms around you, and cradle
Your head forever. Not even a feast survives.
A love poem is like hot food on a table;

No matter how you savor it all, a betrayal
Is inevitable. We must pick up our forks and knives.
I hold you now because I won't be able

To stave off our rupture or live out a fable.
Not that I won't try, with tears in my eyes.
A love poem only mimics food on a table,

The nourishing meal, the daily staple
As it argues beautifully for otherwise.
Hold on to it, till time shows it's unable.
Let's eat, my loves. Food's on the table.

Eye-Broom Sonnet

The salvias in bloom
Were an ante-room
For satiety, an anti-tomb
Where life found air
Singing. I looked for
Something to read
Besides the lawn seed.

So many pages to turn!
(My mind's an eye-broom.)
The cloth was torn
On the north drapes.
I got lost in old maps.
Countries were gone
And I was alone.

Hear Back

Nature, as observed from human nature,
Is like throwing our voice, straight into
The red breast of the robin, the steely eyes
Of the gator, the assessing claws
Of the bear, even the veins of a maple leaf.
From our platform, we're magnified
And spread wide. I've been sitting
On our patio in the canyon with my coffee
And binoculars, watching shadows climb
The desiccated November chaparral,
And hear back, in the shadow of a hawk,
The question with no answer.

Balking, He)

Balking, he
jumped to his death and let his girlfriend
help him back onto the
balcony.

Brain)

Brain,
were you my sanity's prey, not master
of the hunt? Whose blood circles
the drain?

Corrected)

Corrected
grounds for self-esteem, when I discover
the light on my brilliant friends
is reflected.

Self-Portrait for All Our Selves

    Gasping at the glass ceiling of a lake
    A drowner pushes through blue desperation
    To take those first ten breaths of luck
    While on a nearby dock, a family vacation

        Is in full swing with sexy nonchalance.
        Suits cover lungs. A boat is ready to launch.

A tall sail cradles the automatic oxygen
The drowner devours. Gratitude when
The drama is over, dissipates with the wind

    At nightfall. Justice for all. In our sleep,
    Soft breath. Need is not ours to keep.

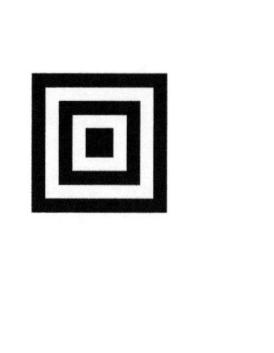

And Now I'm Sane

Now I'm sane,
By most measures.
The sea air
Buoys me again
And I occupy myself
Sorting out treasures
Ferried over
From Asylum Island.

Though my brain
Does not feel
A survivor's command
It comforts me,
My thoughts' couch.
Touch and retouch
The heart, free
Like drawing on sand.

Zoo

We licked each other's wounds,
Slept with backs against the bars.
We drank the water they gave us.
We heard the passing cars.

Then one day I'm free
But I won't be leaving my friends.
They cry with hollow eyes
That say *This is where it ends.*

Now you wear nice clothes
And have a churro in your hand.
No one on the other side
—tsk, tsk, ever understands.

"Take my right hand, Baboon."
But he nearly gnaws it right off.
I lick my own wound.
I taste only the memory of love.

.

Surviving Son As Gravedigger

Yes, I've been filling holes
Since I can remember.

Innocent holes, restoring
Minor missteps or
Dreams to a pat wholeness.
But now the vee-eee words
Come in a tumble: *live,*
Leave, believe, save, grave,
Give, forgive, grieve…

Already I'm shoveling with a sieve.

Energy

       Is genius energy?
—but I'm exhausted, like a deity
  without the synergy

of acolytes. By what rights
      will the gate on the heights
  swing open, the whites

of God's eyes cloudy
     like mine, as close to gray
as *yes* was to *maybe?*

Normy Starts With No

Now decades later, part of the soothing furniture,
I forage for and quickly discard words
That describe the magic that has me by the throat
As my interlocutor bats each away
Heroically, stamped with a diagnosis or at least
A judgment. I'm five defending Santa Claus.
Love, that sodden (once sudden) word that brings
My mouth to violence as easily as victory,
Proves to be a translation device from the way
It is to the way it feels. I can *feel* all manner
Of unformed art in jolting unison waving the white flag,
One that flapped all colors and now
Connotes only surrender to sense and sadness.

Old Patient as the Last of the Great Magazines

The first editor of the magazine would lop
Off the last paragraph of most every story
Submitted to him. Where did those haystacks
Of overzealous phrases go? Did they fall
Through the cracks, develop a drug habit?
Our lives have not been perfect to this point,
At least you can admit that. But amputate
Them just below today's date and they can float
Along on their calm and plotless current,
Like steamboats. You and I mixing it up in
The nonsense of tomorrow.
                                  Or let's forget
The "along," they can bob. Perfect red apples.
Love locked in.

Recipe

Life is eight parts memory

With an expiration date

And one part forgetting in advance.

I am not a cook, so no recipes.

I am not a chemist,

So no solutions. I am a poet, so I leave crumbs

Along this coyote path

And against the advice of history,

I also wear the essence of time.

The recreation of recollection?

Why do we play love, even as the city

Wolves show themselves

To be bored with this rodeo?

It will get dark with or without us

But without us, I won't care.

Isn't That Crazy?

My love was so pure during that summer,
Clarifying like peaceful alpine waters
And knitting tenses together like up- and
Downstream to make a gem of continuity
And yet now I'm supposed to believe it was
All just madness, a disease, a remarkable
Tightrope over a dangerous imbalance. Isn't
There a limit to what can be taken back?
This strain of love, its stain.

See You in the Funny Papers

My heart is filled with phrases
That dazed in their day, words in canny
Order, solving clouds and mazes
Of blundering expression. Company
Is what they keep if not currency:
Quaint as "ain't," jokey as "golly gee,"
They fill a page of antiquated slang
On my screen. Clearly someone young
Compiled it, who had a good laugh
With a friend (someone on the staff
Even junior to them?) *See the freak*
Show! the blog announces, a bleak
Come-on and come-in, as if "bogart"
Were a bearded lady. I want no part
Of this yet feel the pull to extinct
Myself, the past and I sadly linked.

The Snows of No Country

As if I were visiting my old elementary school
And finding the memories spotty as old plaques
Of Kennedy and Kinmont—the beautiful
Ski racer who crashed and paid her death tax

By teaching us kids from a wheelchair—
I trace the thick score of my life's opera.
Some pages cling to each other, worn clear
Here and there to the leaf beneath as if one year is prey

And another its predator. The nothingness
Is Blake's blood, pumping away for purchase
Of recall. Reminiscence is what the nest
Sounds like to the migrating bird. Chase

My portion down as if it were adorned: the high note
Only a lover can bear, a child of the flute.

Spending Lies

But then one recovers, as do the objects
Of one's affection. As in covering
Again. Can recovery be a bad thing?
Side effects, the blight of blasé,
A mild fever of yeah, whatever.
I guess I'm still loving everything
But having to remind myself; my mind-
Ful calm's not sticky anymore.
The thrill isn't gone. It's just shopping
With coupons, putting things back.

Summer Break

I drive by the corner of Venice and Inglewood
Several times a week, and occasionally I cry
Or at least tears well. The boulevard cannot be wide
Enough to contain the breadth of my

Journey nor the difference between clients
And alumni like me. The treatment center
Is behind the bus stop, my reliance
On the place much further. Can't believe I went here.

Stopped at the Inglewood light, I'm like a vase
That's back behind glass on the shelf
Of a museum, fastened securely at my base;
The love that helped me repair myself

Glares off the windshield, hiding me. Every
Time a client (or other human) crosses the street,
I crave contact, as if my recovery
Has cut off the supply. They look straight

Ahead as a rule. I guess I could beep
The horn and make the most
Of the moment, simulate camaraderie I couldn't keep

But inauthenticity is a waterless coast,
Looking is no substitute for seeing,
And only illness can startle love into being.

Canyon Morning

This morning, my ideas dissolve
In the fresh canyon air
Like an Alka-Seltzer. In the pool
My reflection shows the colors
Of my history—all the way back
To those autumns in New York,
The sugar maples in the park where I walked
The dog who died young.
Yes, I was lost then—
Still am, partly—
But there's a spotlight
On my obsolescence now.
There's something to see.

Canyon Market

In the heralded fresh bright blue sky
Of day you can't see a single star,
Unless it's tenancy of memory, or sparkling
From the end of a sharp pencil
Against a lined page. Ripeness is
What our lives stand in line for,
Make lines out of, not the spring of youth
Long before the juicy harvest. Scars
Are the ladder-rungs of desire. Lived-
Through, our complete instructions
From first breath through the last in large
Sweet type. *We're never so young
As before we die* says the sweet peach,
With its kind give.

Glasses, with Bird

Wrentit. "Rented" on Google's
Recording. This tenant pays. My goggles
Can't see through a thicket of trees
Though they can read Dr. See's
Small print. I'm new to perfect
Sight yet it's the hidden nature I dissect
With a poet's joyful belief
That affords me this vision of joy. I laugh
At the Church of I Guess.
I have nothing to confess.

Envoi I

Will we look back
And see we were locked in,
Though we committed
No crime, and locked out, too,
Of many houses?
Perspective, show me
(If you are merciful)
That we locked horns
And honked horns
Because nothing would keep us
From the deep us,
Which we reeled like a fish
Up to the surface,
And watched it flop
Around for a bit
In the bright light.

Envoi 2

I used to have a lot of energy

But somewhere along the way I sprung a leak

And lost my passable physique

But as I waned, I left my lethargy

Behind, like a tankful

Of gas or a full charge of an electric car.

I'm packed to travel; a thankful

Cry like trees make at the end of a war

Is still heard in the provinces

When I ride a train through meadows of Queen Anne's lace

And summer rain rinses

Self-pity from this old man's face.

It hurts to move

But oh how I love

This world, with every neutron, electron, and proton

And now I have you to dote on.

Envoi 3

Who were my summer friends
That appeared stranger the closer
We became? Picture, in chalk,
A flash cross-section, a biopsy
Of random backgrounds plugging
Up blue sky in the atrium
At the center, as if we'd stepped off
An elevator after being stuck
Inside for a month or two, as if
We were just short of eating
One another ... and laughing about it.
Bonds (untouched mortals
Can only imagine) forged in fear,
Of just about everything
But our deepened humanity.
These days I'm smiling more
Broadly, swaying with the palm
Trees. With each trip around
The sun, there's a more profound
Patina on our prospects,
A soul-surface that blinds me
To the limits of setting
Our sights, where each of us
Who had failed to kill
Ourselves learned to live.

Envoi 4

Follow the shadows of things
Patiently, like a Nat Geo photographer,
While the giant ash tree finishes
Its set. The sun breaks into your property.
Bees hop with their e, dropping off
Hope and alight. It's buzzing room only
In the network of salvia bordering
The waterfall and grotto. An accent
Of white butterflies. Exiled monarchs.
When the pair of wrentits up
And exit into the ficus, follow their lead
And retreat. The birds, once real,
Are imagined; fancy begins in earnest.
A blazing sphere of freshened ideas
Casts ever sharper shadows. Every song
Begins in song's absence.

Envoi 5

I wonder, being
One of many
And not a desert
Isle, will you run
With any less
Urgency for the
Plane waiting on
The tarmac?

Envoi 6

Remember carbon
Paper? Whole forests
Do, I'll bet. Sleep
Tonight knowing
I'm on your grocery
List. Notice, darling,
My head is nowhere
Near the pillow.

Envoi 7

I am still waiting for the lion,
Said to pad about
The dense woods
Above our long house
In the canyon.

Said to, sad to employ that phrase.
An admission.
An abdication of power.
An ice cream cone
To almost any day in California.

Envoi 8

You will not kill me until I'm done

I am old but I am bolder for each rung
Of the ladder

Fixed by what I couldn't do
When I was young

No explicit fate
No expiration date for this package of plans
The only thing that freezes in my winter is time

I will not read the writing on the wall
That says my winter is to fall

I have stumbled
As if the ground has rumbled beneath me
Although the Earth is still and I am calm

You will not kill me until I'm done

I have seen the elders sway (It's not okay!)
And heard them sigh (Why oh why?)
When a speaker a third their age takes the stage

When the best page
In a story is always near the end
And a book goes on as long as it wants

I hear your taunts
I hear my own
But you will not kill me until I'm done

I will not be shuttled to the exit door
Like cattle in the abattoir
Like a battle in a losing war

Old feet know best how to take a stand
Old hands how to wield a magic wand

If the world passes me by
It's only because I step aside
And let it.

Just because I have not come into my own yet
Just because I have not flown yet
Does not mean I am not a bird

Writing You Now

It's fragrant here, these flowers left for dead.
My desk's a suspension. I'm in a dark way,
As half of Earth is sad, despite the light ahead.

On social media, even preachers preach
Moderation. Eat cake, but not every day.
Smells wrong. Fear of obsession: Why teach

That to our kids? Abstention empties a bay.
Why, when my life is whole at last, take a break?
To know myself? Not for my heart's sake.

The surf is dogged in its quest to reach
The sand. Sea's apprentice, I request no hours off.
Why should I brook interruption to love?

The Prayer Sonnet

Cumulus, Fog, and Stratus, as you scud,

Tumble and blow, may you guard over poor Maria.

Shelter her. Be a cushion when she falls,

A beacon when she's lost. Answer when she calls.

Keep low. Stay close, like mud

To a shoe, or a reflection to a mirror.

When she stops, either to drink

From the bottle she carries to slake her

Thirst and catch her breath or think

Where this route or that will take her,

Step on your cottony brakes — you're allowed.

Take five to marvel at her lightness,

Mutability, independence, and brightness.

Would she not make a wonderful cloud?

Red-Tailed Hawk

Alone in the backyard, too early to be thinking
Of dinner and too soon to be missing you

This much, I follow the path of the hawk
At the crest of the hill. No, it should be a path,

A hunting trip among the invisible clouds.
But the hawk is not moving, not even its wings

In adjustment to the wind's whim. Neither
Forward, back, up, down, tilt, nor recumbent.

How beautifully God has fashioned its body
For this task, that of prayer and confirmation.

Set Free

Set free, I don't gush like water from a dam.
I don't writhe like a mouse that escapes a sticky trap.
I don't look back like a letter that flees the mother
Alphabet, knowing full well the cost of its decamping.
I collect shells, which I haven't done since

I was a boy, and blind to suffering of this type.
I trace tender ovals on the shiny glaze of this empty
Mussel like I'm stirring time. It's the peaceable
Suspense I feel when I'm in a kitchen alone,
Considering the provenance of an ingredient.

I never know whether I'm older or younger
Than I want to be. Is milk my touchstone, or wine?
I wonder whether my life will rise, a soul-soufflé,
Before I am a shell, too. My knees hurt
Like they know where I'm going, set free.

Acknowledgments

My gratitude to these publications, in which the following poems first appeared, often in different form and/or with a different title.

Abandon Journal	"Envoi 7"
Asses of Parnassus	"Goddess"
The Antioch Review	"Two Harbors"
Beyond Words	"Werewolf"
Commonweal	"Four Moons"
	"Mother Birds"
	"Spending Lies"
	"Not a Week Goes By"
National Review	"A Corto di Eternità"
	"Dolphins On Glass"
	"The Marine Layer"
	"Party of One"
	"The Prayer Sonnet"
	"See You in the Funny Papers"
	"Writing You Now"
The New Criterion	"Set Free"
Nine Muses Poetry	"The Peanut Butter Party"
Palette	"Breathwork"
The Perch	"Balance"
Poetry Ireland Review	"Red-Tailed Hawk"
Rattle (Poets Respond)	"Hard Labor"
The Road Not Taken	"A Forest Tale"
The Stony Thursday Book no.20	"Envoi 4"
Times Literary Supplement	"This Carrier"
Waterwheel Review	"Canyon Market"
Wingless Dreamer	"The Normy Cheer"

Rare Fuel is the winner of the 2023 Donna Wolf-Palacio Poetry Prize from Finishing Line Press.

"Canal Nocturne" was selected for the Knopf anthology, TOGETHER IN A SUDDEN STRANGENESS: America's Poets Respond to the Pandemic.

"Canal Nocturne" was also featured as part of the Hotchkiss Library of Sharon event as well as the Vroman's Live event.

"A Corto di Eternità" is dedicated to Lisa Scottoline and her fine novel, *Eternal*.

"Silver Lining" was an Honorable Mention in the the *Passager* Annual Poetry Contest.

"Silver Lining" was also featured on the "Burning Bright" webcast, hosted by Jon Shorr.

"Two Harbors" was featured on *Poetry Daily*.

A selection of poems from this book was selected as an AWP *Kurt Brown Prize* finalist.

There are several poems here whose titles are followed by a ")". These are written according to the rules of the boomerang, a form I created with the help of the gracious and playful form-lover Richard Wilbur. Essentially, a boomerang is haiku-adjacent. It must be four short lines in length. The first word/sound must at least loosely rhyme with the last word/sound, which makes the poem uncannily symmetrical. Wilbur thought to make the first and last lines shortest, and to emulate the path and energy-journey of a boomerang. In his words, you're riffing off "a thrown boomerang [which] has three phases: it flies to first base (as it were), then travels over to third and rises, then swoops home." The parenthesis in the title, mainly for fun, emulates a physical boomerang.

Rex Wilder is the author of four books of acclaimed poetry and *Rare Fuel* is his fifth, winner of the Donna Wolf-Palacio Poetry Prize from Finishing Line Press. Stephanie Burt, whom the New York Times calls "one of the most influential poetry critics of her generation," writes: "You can place [*Rare Fuel*] alongside the language's other great verse chronicles of madness: Christopher Smart, say, or Ivor Gurney." Andrew McCulloch, upon choosing a Wilder piece for the TLS Poem of the Week," explains his enthusiasm: "As Larkin once said, 'every poem starts out as either true or beautiful. Then you try to make the true ones seem beautiful, and the beautiful ones true.' When she described Wilder's poetry as both "worldly and otherworldly", Stephanie Burt pointed to his success in achieving this combination of beauty and truth. In terms of tone and technique, too, Wilder straddles wide divides—he has been praised by poets as different as Richard Wilbur and Billy Collins, and was described by Burt as 'a cross between Ashbery and Wordsworth.'" Wilder is also a fine-art photographer and mental health advocate. Currently he is Board Chair of The Maple Counseling Center in Los Angeles. He lives outside L.A. in the Hollywood Hills with his human family, dog family, and occasional curious mule deer.

Milton Keynes UK
Ingram Content Group UK Ltd.
UKHW030956261124
451585UK00005B/708